Up in
Space

Jupiter

and

Saturn

Rosalind Mist

QED Publishing

Editor: Lauren Taylor
Designer: Melissa Alaverdy
Educational consultants:
    Heather Adamson
    and Jillian Harker

Copyright © QED Publishing,
2013

First published in
the UK by QED Publishing,
A Quarto Group Company
230 City Road,
London EC1V 2TT

www.qed-publishing.co.uk

ISBN 978 1 78171 212 2

Printed in China

A catalogue record for this
book is available from the
British Library.

Picture credits
(fc=front cover, t=top,
b=bottom, l=left, r=right,
c=centre)

NASA NSSDC 1t, Hubble
Heritage Team (STScI/AURA)
1b, 2-3, 4-5, 10-11, 11b, 16-17,
NSSDC 17t
Science Photo Library
NASA 11t, JPL/Space Science
Institute 12-13, JPL-Caltech
13t, JPL/Space Science
Institute 14-15, 18-19, 22-23,
NASA 22-23
Shutterstock Njaj 4-5, 6-7,
Sabino Parente 8-9, keren-
seg 10-11, Computer
Earth 19t, eddtoro 20-21,
cobalt88 24

Words in bold
appear in the
Glossary on
page 24

Contents

Jupiter

Jupiter is the largest planet in the **Solar System**. It is the fifth planet from the **Sun**. Jupiter is bigger than all the other planets put together.

Earth

Jupiter is mainly
made of gas.

The Solar System

The Solar System is made up of the Sun and everything that moves around it.

Sun

Earth

Mercury

Venus

Neptune

Uranus

Saturn

Jupiter

Mars

A force called **gravity** holds the Solar System together. We cannot see gravity.

Days and years

Jupiter spins very fast even though it is big. A day on Jupiter is only 10 hours, but a year on Jupiter is as long as 12 Earth years!

daytime

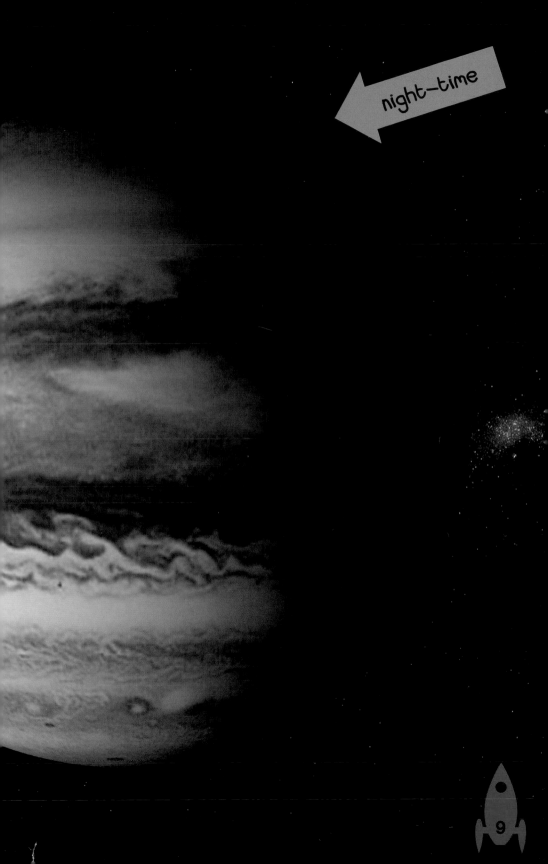

night-time

Jupiter's moons

Jupiter has at least 63 moons. They are all different sizes. Io is the closest large moon to Jupiter.

Io has a lot of **volcanoes**. It is brightly coloured.

Io

Jupiter

Europa

Callisto

Ganymede

Cloudy planets

Jupiter and Saturn look like huge clouds. They spin so fast that their clouds line up in coloured bands.

Jupiter

The coloured bands make the planets look like they have stripes.

Great Red Spot

The Great Red Spot on Jupiter is a huge storm. It has lasted for over 300 years.

The red swirl of clouds is more than three times the size of the Earth.

Great Red Spot

Saturn

Saturn is the sixth
planet from the Sun.
Like Jupiter, it is
mainly made of gas.
Saturn is the second
largest planet in the
Solar System.

Saturn is so big that 763 Earths could fit inside it.

Saturn's rings

Saturn has **rings**. The rings are made of millions of rock and ice chunks. The rock and ice may have come from **comets, asteroids** and moons. They broke up when they got too close to the planet.

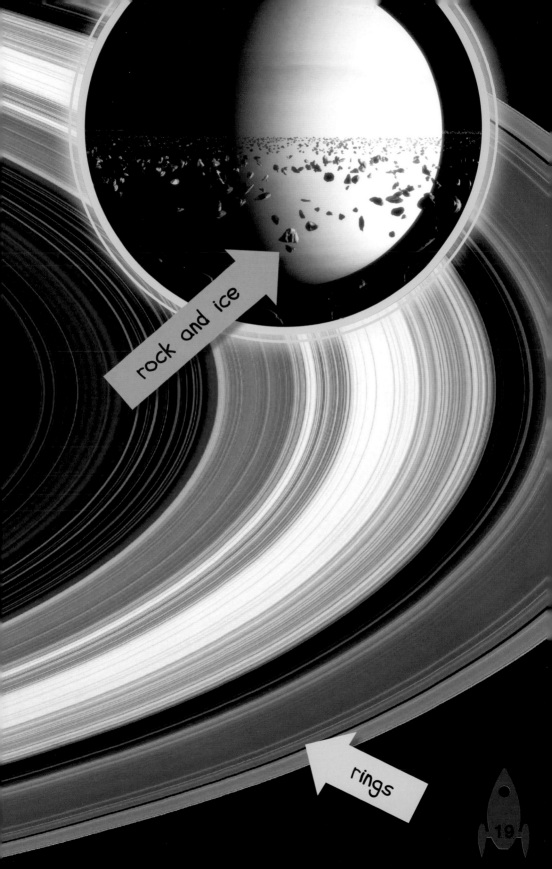

rock and ice

rings

spinning fast

Saturn spins so fast that it is not round like a ball. It is bigger around the middle. This makes it look like it is squashed.

It takes about 10 hours for Saturn to spin once.

Titan

Saturn has at least 60 moons. Its largest moon is called Titan.

Titan

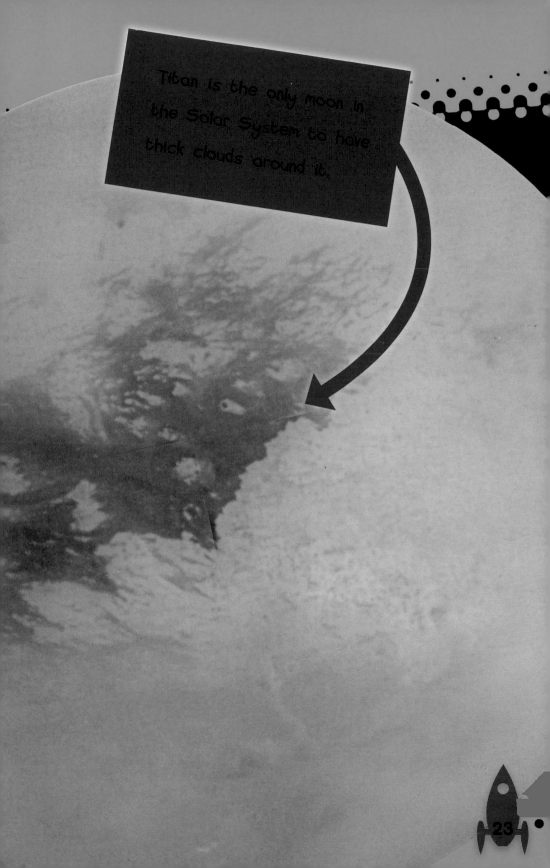

Titan is the only moon in the Solar System to have thick clouds around it.

23

Glossary

asteroids – small rocky objects that move around the Sun

comet – a chunk of ice and dirt that moves around the Sun in a long path

gravity – the force that pulls things towards each other

moon – a natural object that moves around a planet

planet – one of the eight large objects circling the Sun

rings – bands of dust and small rocky pieces that orbit some planets

Solar System – the Sun and all of the things that move around it

Sun – the star that the Earth and the planets move around

volcano – a mountain through which melted rock, ash and hot gases sometimes erupt